Paradoxides

Paradoxides

Poems

Don McKay

McClelland & Stewart

Published simultaneously in the United States of America by McClelland & Stewart Ltd., P.O. Box 1030, Plattsburgh, New York, 12901

LIBRARY AND ARCHIVES CANADA CATALOGUING IN PUBLICATION

McKay, Don, 1942–
Paradoxides / Don McKay.

Poems.

ISBN 978-0-7710-5509-6

I. Title.

PS8575.K28P37 2012   C811'.54   C2011-904425-0

Library of Congress Control Number: 2011931127

We acknowledge the financial support of the Government of Canada through the Book Publishing Industry Development Program and that of the Government of Ontario through the Ontario Media Development Corporation's Ontario Book Initiative. We further acknowledge the support of the Canada Council for the Arts and the Ontario Arts Council for our publishing program.

Typeset in Aldus by M&S, Toronto
Printed and bound in Canada

This book was produced using ancient-forest friendly paper.

McClelland & Stewart Ltd.
75 Sherbourne Street
Toronto, Ontario
M5A 2P9
www.mcclelland.com

1   2   3   4   5   16   15   14   13   12

For Marlene

CONTENTS

As If   1

I

Song for the Song of the Canada Geese   5
Slow Spring on Vancouver Island   6
Song for the Song of the Sandhill Crane   7
Forlorn   8
Song for the Song of the Common Loon   10
Ravens at Play over Mount Work   11
Juncos   13
Song for the Song of the Purple Finch   14

II

On the Barrens   17
Alias Rabbit, Alias Snowshoe Hare   19
Porch   21
Sleeping with the River   23
Batter –   24
Eddy Out   26
Apparition   29
Sleeping Places   31

III

Deep Time Encounters   35
Labradorite   36
Mistaken Point   38
Paradoxides   39
    Cephalon   39
    Thorax   41
    Pygidium   43
Tuff   44
Snowball Earth   46
Rock Flour   48
Crinoid   49
Gjall   50
The Wopmay Orogen: a field trip   51

IV

Thingamajig   55
    To Clasp   57
    To Step   63
    To Rock   67

V

Taking the Ferry   73
Descent   77

Notes   79
Acknowledgements   85

Paradoxides

AS IF

spirit vigor (handwritten)

metrical foot (handwritten, left margin)

Play it con brio, a muscular
iamb, a frisbee sizzling –
_as if_ – into no man's land,
an emptiness unfurling fast and
fernlike. Last winter, from a cliff
along the coast, I saw a Milky Way
strewn lavishly across the cove,
twinkling in the chop.
It was cold, and so
some moments before my stiff fingers
unburied the binoculars and found it

large seaduck (handwritten, left margin)

to be eiders. In their black skipper's caps
they scudded the waves, cold's own creatures,
their white chests flashing in the slant sun,
until, as at a signal, with a move
part gulp, part slurp, each, one after the other,
dove, like this: as if, as if, as
if that surface were the border –
suddenly porous –
between yes and no, so
and not so.

I

SONG FOR THE SONG OF THE CANADA GEESE

Something of winter, something of winter
again, something of that famous mortal reed
making an oboe of the throat.
As though the soul – not
so much in pain as under pressure –
yelped. Angst,
angst, bite-sized bits of loneliness sent
back to the heartless skies
they fell from, giving grief
its rightful place among the elements.
                                        So what
if they waddle, shit
gooseshit on the grass all summer then neglect
to migrate? Were the geese to quit
their existential yammer, talk
would also cease, each would-be dialogue collapse
into its own hole. Where there was ivy,
ice. Ice
where there was moss.
                        All praise to the geese
in their goosiness, to the ragged arrow that is
and isn't eros.

[handwritten annotations: "lowest below the forest canopy" above "understory"; "lower voice for emphasis" above "sotto voce"]

In the understory, *sotto voce,*
crypto-birds rehearse. Is
that you, Junco,
setting your Hopkins-self aside
to sip-sip-sip so
generically? That you, Varied Thrush,
clearing your throat ad
nauseum, uncertain
as the rain that quits, dithers,
threatens, finally
compromises on the drizzle into which
your indecipherable ciphers fit like inter-
office memoranda?
                              Over the dun
duff of the forest floor one alder leaf –
thinned by winter to its skeleton –
hangs like a glyph.
Foliose lichens urge their hypergreens.
One day soon –
so goes the tale – Junco's voice
will quicken into trill, its quick lusts
gargling. Varied Thrush
will thrust its whistle-hum
frankly into the mix, and that last leaf –
like an icon suddenly
relaxing to cliché –
uncling. And then – by
the Jesus we'll be on our way.

It eschews the ear,
with its toolshed, its lab, its Centre for Advanced
Studies in Hermeneutics and Gossip,
to boom exactly in my thorax,
rattling the bones and waking the baby. Garroo:
the *o*'s are caves of lunar gravity, the rolled *r*
recalls the ratchet of life and death.
Why am I standing on this frigid porch
in my pyjamas, peering into the mist
that rises in little spirals from the pond?
Where they call from the blue
has nearly thinned to no-colour-
clear. Where
they call from hominids haven't yet
happened. Garroo:
who can bear those star-river distances?
I'm so lonesome I could die
happy.

The very word is, if
you ask me, like a horn –
fog, French, krumm, *cor
anglais*, or car – depending on the timbre
and accent of its native loss.
It's never like the bell
that tolled Keats back to life the night
he nearly OD'ed on The Nightingale.
Anyway, what odds? It tolls
for him but honks for me, a closed nasal
existential echo, not quite
recovered from that nasty cold.
                              Forlorn:
the bare unfaeried self re-pots us
in our deaths as into humus.
Not *lonely*, twanging of teen angst
and Nashville. Not *solitary*,   – monk-
with its would-be-Thomas-Merton air
of being the best graduate student He
has supervised in eras.
                              Forlorn:
it is 2:45 a.m.
again. Noises, some like itch,
some like scratch, surround the cabin.
One rises in a hiss
(snake? bird? cat?) over
and over until I'm up, irascible,
up and out, dammit, with the flashlight

stumbling toward the source.
As though whatever it is
started to say "curse" then
switched to "kiss,"
then "ship." The flashlight poking tunnels
into the dark, selecting arty angles
through the foliage, and finds them – there,
huddled on a branch, two grey lumps,
staring down the beam like fluffy
wide-eyed monks. Owlets,
I'm guessing barred, out of the nest
but not yet fledged, still
begging for food from the ruthless mother,
who is elsewhere. *growing darkness*
        Darkling, I listen,
switching off the spot. The hiss
of hunger, separation, and – to insert
a personal note – sleeplessness. *Ksship*:
how to translate that?
            Forlorn, of course,
the very word.

SONG FOR THE SONG OF THE COMMON LOON

If that's the word:
the song's already gone
before it's uttered so the ear is left
full of its emptiness,
bereft.
        It seems the loon
opens its throat to some old
elemental wind, it seems that time
has finally found a syrinx and for a moment
lets itself be voice.

What perilous music!
Surely, like Odysseus, we ought
to stop our ears against this feral ultrasound
with its dreadful
diagnostic reverb? But no,
we would rather be stricken, rather suspect
that the spirit also is a migratory species,
that it is right now flying to Star River –
as the ancients called the Milky Way – that
in fact it is already there,
yodelling for no one and ignoring us,
the collectors, with our heads full of closets,
our hearts full of ovens,
and our sad feet.

The power dive, the clash-and-roll, the steep
veer that limns the knife edge
hidden in the wind, the proto-
contrapuntal game of tag:
                         this is the improv
at the heart of things, this stirring up
of trouble, this festival of riffs.
They jam until the air
is pregnant with polyphony, with Scott
LaFaro meets Bill Evans, do-si-
do meets alley-oop I love you Abbott
and Costello, flirt with Escher, flirt with
Jackson Pollock, hold the moment in your wingpit, then
buckle, fold, toss yourself like a crumpled draught
and come to roost.
                    To make the spirits
envious. To make them laugh. What if
we snuck up on the minuet
and goosed it with this jalapeño?
What if we stole those thick
black eels that live inside despair
and ate them like electrical
spaghetti? *Yowp.* Such schemes they
palaver in Polyglot, having scavenged Yiddish,
Irish, !Kung, English, and
Inuktitut. Intro-
aggroverts of small-b being,
they can project a *kark* across the Malahat or swallow it –

glug – like a melancholy
clock. Glottal stop,
glottal glide, doorbell
crossed with oboe, oboe
crossed with short-eared owl. *Tók.*
To make the spirits
give themselves away.
With a rustle of wings like a whispered
death wish one of them swings
down to check me out,
perched on the summit writing
yowp, writing *tók* and *wörk*, writing what
would it be like to be so casual and acute
in my little blue notebook filled with
phrases, numbers, recipes,
and to-do lists.

JUNCOS

Where "shades of grey" acquires
esprit: slaty, dark-eyed,
sooty, dapper, hooded –
quick bits of dusk stitching fir
to birch to rock the boreal
embroidery.
              All winter
they animate the understory, inscribing
runic ciphers in the snow
and discrete diacritical *chips*
along their flight paths.
                          One oriole,
it is said, can shift the heart
into its own outcry.
But it's the juncos,
in their undertaker outfits,
who slip unnoticed into melancholy
smuggling minims of lift.

Bless them. They exit
with a wink, tail
snapping open like a card hand to reveal
white feathers at each edge:
                          Come spring
they'll find the tallest spines of spruce
and trill the sun from one
saw-toothed horizon to the other.

Honey, if you had some of this in a carafe
you could mix yourself a comic opera out of
willow willow willow, chemotherapy, and
washing your socks in the sink.
Know what I mean? I mean what-is is
perched on the precipice where chat
breaks into song or it may be laughter
breaking into Welsh or Aunt Clara's pure
lyrical harangue breaking like combers over
Uncle Archie in her kitchen. I mean life
for sure is tragic but honey you
aren't. Here's your purple guitar. Adios.

II

ON THE BARRENS

Ghost-grey, tipsy in its V,
the harrier hovers, wavers,
glides, an ever-adjusting
motion sensor scanning the crowberry-
cranberry-blueberry-goowiddy-
bottlebrush-tuckamore
tapestry below, then, angling sharply,
sideslips out of sight
and into someone's near
or sudden death.

I lower the binoculars,
craving the dwarf subspecies
of myself, like the sideways birch
crawling the outcrop, or the fir
whose one-way branches obey the wind,
even when, as now,
it's gone off somewhere to replenish huff.

To be fit
means to be in shape but also
to be shaped by the weather's
rough injustice. Means
grow tensile, grow vines

to hyphenate with neighbours
and resist. Means thin
the spirit, or,
if that isn't spirit, then
whatever it is that's whet
and spare and whisky-fierce within.

ALIAS RABBIT, ALIAS SNOWSHOE HARE

All winter we watch for a clear night
with a full moon, when we will head off
into the woods to wait,

standing on contraptions that mimic, stiffly,
your long spring-loaded paws.
The sparse spruce will cast shadows

so black they fall right through the earth
into infinity. Between them the moonlight
will mix with the snowlight as the ghosts

of a mother and her daughter who at last
embrace. And after we have stood a while
with the cold speaking in their own tongue

to our bones, you will leap across our path
in effortless arcs, white on white on black
on white, each spring a fluid coiling-up of power

for the next. As you exit
we'll be left with your afterimage,
and the cold, and the flask of twelve-year-old

Macallan in the backpack. But for now
we watch the weather and the calendar
and read about you in the library,

and eat you, with mushrooms, onions, and a little sherry
in the stew, and follow your asymmetrical prints,
hind feet bounding past the fore, and once

we come upon the strike, a sudden full stop
where an owl has gathered up your
story into hers, and we wonder,

once again, if that night will ever come
when our path crosses yours, either up
in the country or down in some deep

articulate midwinter dream.

PORCH

The tractor harrowing one farm over
coughs and quits. Now there's only tree frogs
and the thin half-moonlight pewtering the leaves
and glinting off the fender of the rental.
The tree frogs chant in phase, then out,
then in, as though composed by Philip Glass.
I've read that Lao Tzu,
leaving community for wilderness,
paused at the border, where the guard asked
for some record of his teachings.
So: the *Tao de Ching*. The thin line
between lost past and dim future opens
into an evening and a porch
on which to rock and listen,
listen and rock. Lao Tzu's actual existence –
the path-following, border-crossing one –
is, so I've also read,
doubtful, like Robin Hood's and Homer's.
In close-up, and in memory,
the tree frog wasn't really credible,
a translucent elf from some outer space,
splayed, finger pads extended,
on the porch screen. I gaped at it;
it gaped into the wide night.
The tao that can be spoken

is not the true Tao: so the sage,
who probably did not exist, and with
exquisite paradox, began.
I slipped off to fetch the camera
and when I got back it was gone.

All that winter as the rains arrived,
sometimes as nobody's footsteps,
sometimes ack-ack, sometimes
hard bits of Braille flung at the house,
the mailbox, the woodshed, at the car parked
in the driveway, at all that is solid, all
that winter leaving the window open to its
pizzicati, hearing them accelerate and blend and
drown in the river's big
ambiguous chorus, all that winter being
swept asleep thinking river is only rain
that has its act together, song that has never
passed through speech, unschooled,
other-than-us, thinking
this must be the voice of what-is as it
seizes the theme, pours its empty opera,
pumps out its bass line of sea-suck and blues.

BATTER –

that's the name, I'm thinking,
for the huff-and-buffet
rhetoric that fulminates against me, me
and every other smart-arsed upstart
lover-of-the-vertical who ventures
up on the tolt it scours
and sculpts. Across Conception Bay it gathers wrath
and hurls it, a tirade so pauseless,
so pressure-hosed that listening's impossible
and mandatory, the poor mind veering King
Learily into synch, unbonneted,
banging back and forth like bad hockey.
Already, in deference, I've doffed
and packed away my hat and glasses, now
it wants me bare and walking-stickless,
wants me smeared like flesh-and-calcium pâté
across the rough volcaniclastic ridge.
To catch my breath I crouch
in the lee of an impeccably poised
erratic, an elephant *en pointe*, CFA,
emplaced by a glacier with a raven's
drastic sense of humour.
In a moment, once I've regathered mass
and gravity, I will arise and lurch
up onto the crest, heading, with my
squat-hunched stagger, for the shelter
of that patch of tuckamore –

the bristling ancient quasimodoed
hedgehog of a life form
that lives here.

EDDY OUT

Late fall, rain so thorough
everyone is glad it's not the snow
it is, so says the radio,
in Happy Valley-Goose Bay.
It sheets the study window
and sets the sump pump
humming in the basement.
Something in me,
nameless and familiar, stirs,
unsettles, flaps into action like a one-winged
gull. How many winters more
before I seamlessly shift, a snowshoe hare's fur
passing into white?
Beware an idle wish,
I tell myself, and don't go plunging into snow tire–
firewood–long john frenzy either. No,
this is the time to summon old
warm-blooded silences, air pockets that hold heat
and buoyancy at once. Not stories, mind,
but their pauses, strung like the bladders
on a long frond of kelp.
Without them, a lifeline
shrinks to bio, c.v.,
obit. Deaf
to the cupped hush between the winter wren's
cadenzas. Immune
to our own music's held breath,
when it swims in its underworld

and we wait in safe
aesthetic anguish.
                    So I call up that time –
remember? – late, after "Goodnight, Irene," guitars
back in their cases and gutbucket set aside,
the kids and dogs exhausted,
when we dwindled outdoors to find ourselves
under an hysterical sky, aurora
shooting in aqua sheets, an ice cap
suffering a migraine. As though we'd stepped,
like inattentive tourists, or Duncan Campbell Scott
on one of his imperial canoe trips,
into Norval Morrisseau's medicine.
                              That one.
And later, when I woke my daughter,
carried her outside and pointed up,
feeling like a man exposing photo-sensitive
paper. And still another when,
next day at brunch,
she remembered nothing til I asked
if she'd had any interesting dreams,
and her eyes turned in, and fish
were swimming in them, and she said, "Oh
that."
                    That.
How words, grown corporate or brash,
crave respite from themselves,
how they long to open,
ooid as an aging mooseprint,
into unfamiliar vowels.
                    As the rain,

like a conversation turning mean,
slides into sleet, I eddy out
into those pauses – uterine, caesural,
mammal. Hold them, memory,
breathe fresh air into their emptinesses
while they keep my heavy
history-laden life
afloat.

Then, snow tires.

Half an hour following, on faith,
the car's blunt nose and the fog's become
the stuff that ghosts are made of, and,
off duty, fade back into. Gauze,
mothwing, vagueness, cliché,
inkling: what half-formed spirit will it usher
into our little séance as we creep
our creepy way across the barrens?
But then, as if to show it could concoct acute
as readily as nebulous – what?
                We lurch to the verge:
      foxes.
Four of them, dawdling, hanging out, doglike,
catlike, this one scratching an ear, that one
nipping a sibling in faux-fierce combat,
taking their talent for granted.
Who could invent a creature
that lallygags with such élan?
                Now and then
one glances over, curious, I guess,
about this fog-conjured audience,
and weighing the merits of a Hyundai Sonata
as a source of food or fun.
Inside it we are rapt, two feedback loops
poured into the binoculars and re-imbibed
as sharpness – ear, paw, whisker,
nose. Then something offstage calls
and, like that, three vanish,

gone like luck.
Only the brindled kit
side-trots up the verge,
its lavish brush floated like applause
as though that pent wit
bloomed, what
is this thing called love,
anyway? It dives
into the alders and we sit,
ignition off, attending to whatever else
the fog might slip from those
supposedly empty sleeves.

SLEEPING PLACES

Nature loves to hide
— Herakleitos

What is nothing doing,
there in the pressed grass,
there in the bent-over reeds,
in the slightly scuffed ground
and four-leaved cruciform
bunchberries? Something whispers here
so softly it's dissolving
even as the camera clicks:
catch-and-release, it says, place
is gesture, is delible, the rumple of a moose-bed,
the bower left by lovers, the punched strike
printed by a hunting owl in snow –
a punctuation mark whose sentence has flown off,
the faint strokes left by its wings
already fading. It says
this memory is earth's,
not ours. Relinquish the plot. Uncuff
the hero, his precious flaw, his gift-wrapped
catastrophe. Release the crime scene
television loves, with its frame
of yellow tape, its splayed,
awkwardly outlined corpse nicknamed The Vic

and sentenced to publicity.
Let them slip –
    practise this –
       slip –
back to the unwritten:
      that place where place
sleeps, where sleep itself
seeps into the landscape, having scrawled
in the pressed grass, in the bent-over reeds
its auto-erasing name.
What is nothing doing? The antique
riddle. The old
ungettable joke.

III

There is no silence in the world
Like the silence of the rock before life was
   – Robert Hass

Every dose is overdose,
every thing that's done's
done to death.
Good old ineffability –
that fine froth, that gossamer cliché –
runs amok and bites you, *there*,
somewhere secret, somewhere
in the ancient backstreets of the brain
where pleasure and pain promiscuously
mix. Ordinary stone
turns to the time it's made of,
each empty *O* a lens,
and *why is there not nothing* arcs,
its first full dolphin,
through the mind's stunned air.
Long pause.   Well?
Then that depopulated silence.
That darker dark.

Frostbitten light; shy
hologram; oil spill
practising za-zen.
Always inward, always
aslant, and in that sense
reflective. Awry.
Spirit beings of aurora borealis,
say the Inuit, remain
trapped in the rock, still
dancing the dancerless dance.
Not as diamond,
flashing superlatives, nor acute quartz
singing the rhombohedral madrigal
called amethyst. My field guide
says its schiller rhymes
with the Morpho butterfly's intense
prismatic blue.
       But I wonder:
something in that glance is fell
and full of darkness, the *duende*
of The Land God Gave to Cain,
as though in that moment it were
stalking a possible Persephone.
             To me
it seems that all the elegies
I haven't written wait, not
patiently, inside otherwise plain
plagioclase feldspar. In my kitchen

a small slab serves as trivet, its bronze-
blue phenocrysts winking at the coffee pot
and jam jar. And me,
silently disputing with my dear
difficult departed ones.

As in a genteel living room,
a sterile lab, or mosque,
we have doffed our boots,
and pad across this rock slab
in the sky-blue booties supplied.
Around us, mist.
Underfoot, petrified deep time rises in welts
to prod our soles, here and there
breaking into sudden bas-relief:
a fernlike creature, a creature
like a picket fence, a shrub, a miniature
Christmas tree, a pizza disk – preserved,
like Pompeii, under the cushion of volcanic ash
that killed them. Earth's earliest animals,
says the brochure, Precambrian, pre–Burgess Shale,
five hundred and sixty million – but as usual
my mind is boggling, Googling vainly in the Zenosphere,
finally it files this in a shoe box, taped shut,
and tagged like a rogue elk's ear,
somewhere near infinity.
                              Back here,
in the Anthropocene, South Avalon, July, the mist
is thickening to drizzle. The bedrock darkens,
deepening the contrast. What shall we call
this antique frond, part fern, part feather,
part Art Nouveau and brand new Braille,
urgent and enigmatic as an oracle?

Cephalon

On the day we found the trilobite and took its photograph, we
had already been to visit the gannet colony at Cape St. Mary's, so
you can imagine us picking our way along the foreshore below
the cliffs with thought balloons over our heads, and in each a
scribble of elliptical flight paths, orbits left by the gannets wheeling
around the nucleus of their tall nesting rock. Imagine their black-
tipped wings like long sensitive scythes, their stretched necks
faintly yellow as though dusted with pollen. From a distance,
their cacophony resembles the ratchet ratchet of an old threshing
machine; closer up it's *more more more*, or maybe *here here here*,
the urgent, impacted birth-and-death cries of beings who will,
once departed from their home rock, be mute. The place dense with
energy, taboo, as though we'd stepped inside an atom, chaos and
order in tense standoff, calling directly into the open ear of our
DNA: the sort of place where beauty teeters giddily on the brink
of terror.

So it was a relief to let that potency recede, to embrace an
ordinary walk and contemplate something as quotidian as lunch.
We ambled along the cliff bottom, clambering over squarish blocks
of rubble, strolling the flat water-smoothed shale – some russet
red, some blue grey – which sloped into the sea. There's a lustre
rising in the shale that, were it flesh, we'd call a blush, since it
suggests some inward softening, some memory or hope coming
to the surface. And, although the ocean's wash-and-withdraw
was a constant reminder, it was hard to imagine that water had
transformed the rough cliff without some answering agent, some

reciprocal hankering after smoothness. Eros, erosion. So it seems.

We sat on those smooth boulders to have trail bars and tea. And then, a few paces away, we spotted the trilobite sprawling in the shale – bold, declarative, big as my hand and just as complicated. It seemed the shale had suddenly broken into literacy, publishing one enigmatic pictograph from a secret alphabet. Suddenly it was refusing relegation to raw material. Suddenly it was demanding to be read.

Thorax

For they are local and exotic

For they anticipate lobsters, the Pre-Raphaelites, the tenor saxophone, and the buckskin jacket

For they are *seemingly absurd though perhaps well founded*

For they appear like a fully accoutred medieval knight stepping onto a nearly empty stage

For they are elegant and monstrous

For their pleural spines extend past the thorax *like the kind of drooping moustaches sported by bad guys in westerns*

For they are local and exotic

For *the paradox is the source of the thinker's passion, and the thinker without a paradox is like a lover without feeling*

For they index both the micro-continent of Avalonia and the Mid-Cambrian Period and so situate us in space and time

For they dislocate space

For they infinitize time

For *the immense odds against its occurrence in the rock record*

For hexagonal calcite eyes, which evolution never happened
   on again

For they pose the problems of mind and body
                        nature and culture
                        rock and stone
                        substance and accident
                        mysticism and materialism
                        allochthon and autochthon
                        dressed and overdressed
five hundred million years before the first false dichotomy appears
   in the Anthropocene

For they mean yet do not speak or write

For they are elegant and monstrous

For sometimes I hear *the mind my former lives all share.*

Pygidium

You pose on my desk in the photograph,
a riddle, an odalisque, a rune,
one plump cipher from a long-gone
semiotic system. Cryptic and Sapphic,
at once emerging from the stone
and scuttling into it, you earn
each micro-quantum of the consternation
promised by your name. The more I learn
about you and your family – e.g.,
your eyes were calcite crystals, spars of rock
arranged to transmit light, unique
in all of animalia – the more piquant
your present absence. Friend, stranger, paradoxidid,
I wave one jointed arm.
                    I wink one endothermic lid.

Orts, scraps, coughs, dust, draughts,
ejectamenta of the earth,
unite: such is the call of tuff,
which is to ash as Che
to *campesino*, making mountains
out of next-to-nothings.
Call it igneous,
since born of fire, sedimentary,
for its packed glued particles,
or even metamorphic for a lifeline
that out-Ovids Ovid.
Hot cumulous dust clouds
boil into the stratosphere to cool, recall
their humble roots and fall, layer
upon layer, the planet snowing its own
ashes on itself. Then to be tamped,
pressed by the weight of eons
into toughness, stressed strained
sheared uplifted folded faulted by
tectonic force; eroded by rain;
cracked by frost; rearranged
by glaciers.
                    Nothing never ends,
it says, catastrophe accumulates, the lost
decline to stay lost and return
like dying and reviving rock bands.
Who needs ghosts when matter
nonchalantly haunts us?

The summer before last
we shifted a big tuff boulder up the river,
heaved, levered, nudged it inch by inch,
to make a footing for the bridge.
Drilling holes for bolts,
we dribbled water on the Carborundum bit
and wore down several.
After, the ash at the bottom of each hole
was grey-white, fine as talc, and smelt
like a match you'd just blown out.

SNOWBALL EARTH

1.
Once, way back when,
winter won.
Earth was hard as iron,
water like a stone for something like one
hundred million years. Persephone
must have been depressed,
and postponed all her travel plans
indefinitely. The long commute. The stress
of being sexy and bipolar, bouncing gloom
to joie de vivre to gloom the same
old same old volleyball. Enough.
She settled down to life with grim
ultramafic Death.
                        Up on Earth
the glaciers grew to ice caps, snow
on snow, the ice caps to ice fields,
ice prairies, pampas, veldts, albedo
ramped to the max, Sun's
billets-doux returned to space unread.

So much for that biosphere,
some passing astral being might have said,
inert and gorgeous, a dead movie star,
a tempting but inedible meringue.
                        And they'd be wrong
in the long term. Why? Let all who dwell
on the blue-green planet celebrate

the mother magma churning at its heart,
the home fires that kept burning and at length undid
that cold Precambrian spell.

2.
In the middle of the frozen pond
we pause: blow noses;
tighten snowshoes. Around us

snowdevils skirmish and disperse.
Loose tresses sift, braiding, un-
braiding, and where

the ice is bare the slant sun,
like a glass eye,
glances. Biology is elsewhere,

busy with its death-birth
buzz. Here we are simple citizens
of Snowball Earth, the cosmic disco ball

and nun. Listen: : that mix
of hush and scratch is time
clocklessly elapsing. In a minute

our mammal-selves will come back
bearing tales of frostbite
and heartbreak. For now

just winter pre-echoing the infinite.

ROCK FLOUR

Far off, from the highway,
it seemed just road dust
raised by construction. Closer,
it became a tattered curtain
drawn between two bare black St. Elias
mountains, then a dirty grey
disorderly parade of ghosts
descending from the ice field on its
katabatic wind.
                    Loess
said the guide in the interpretive centre,
rock that's been milled and
remilled by a glacier to a silt so fine
it flies on a whisper. Loss
with its *o* pinched
like the half-closed hole on a flute.
                              Où
sont les roches d'antan? I thought
as I looked back, and down,
from the shoulder of Sheep Mountain.
Ask the motes of the air.
Ask Kluane Lake,
whose milky blue-green tinge
is light plus loess plus water.
Ask the short-faced bear, whose bones
lie buried in Beringia's
surprisingly fertile plain.

CRINOID

A fossil, preposterous
and common, light
as a dime, as infinity's
poker chip, a grey
Tylenol-sized disk you can
slip into your pocket
or cup in your palm.
Turn it on end,
you can see where a delicate fish line
ran down its core. Reel it in,
you'll haul up Ordovician oceans
where they boogied and grew, vertebrae
with frondlike arms and bloomlike heads
asway in the tide that fed them, as the mind
of Wang Wei in the ever-adjusting
wind.
  O Chordates, you'll exclaim
to our distinguished many-membered phylum,
spare a moment to applaud
this alien flowering spine.
      O Elvis,
wherever you are,
shake with the snakes that first
shook it.

Among the many forms into which lava may harden – cinders, tubes, columns, ash, pumice, glass – this one seems the least doctrinaire, the least likely to endorse the orthodox axiom that A is A. Light in the hand, already half in love with other elements, it bears swirls that resemble flickers of flame, and blobs like the congealed drops on the outside of a paint can. Inside, it is packed with vessicles, and sometimes with large smooth-sided hollows like the inside of a nutshell. It might be the material pelt of a burst bubble or the chrysalis left behind when some rock-moth hatched and flew off.

Other igneous rocks – gabbro, granite – identify themselves as citizens of deep time, and remain its devout parishioners. Gjall joins us in history, already wearing the insignia of shift that others will later have thrust upon them by the soft persistence of erosion. "The turnings of fire," says Herakleitos, "first sea, but of sea half is earth, half lightning storm." When it flew from the volcano it was as phlegm, rock froth, the equivalent of ocean spray that leaves salt-suds like grounded clouds snagged in the driftwood and alders. Now it lies among the burnt-out rubble of the lava field, testimony that negative capability is possible even for rocks, that there is no quarter of the perplexed earth not afflicted with longing.

THE WOPMAY OROGEN: A FIELD TRIP

Because it's there.
   – George Mallory

Expect to see the absences
of many alps, their peaks
humbled to tundra. Also the roots
of cold volcanoes, plus the adjacent rocks
they cooked, then the many-faulted, flattened
fold-and-thrust belt, and even the descendants
of molasse deposited offshore. In short
a tale of drastic rise and fall,
like "Ozymandias" or Freytag's Pyramid,
or Gibbon.
            Every valley, Isaiah said,
shall be exalted, and every mountain
and hill laid low. So also fine Old
Testament hyperbole shall be made mundane
as the Weather Channel's forty per cent
probability of showers.
                        All this
shall be raised up again
on the exam. Answers
may be carved in granite, writ
on water, or delivered as a lecture
to the air. Because it was, because it is,
because it isn't there.

IV

There are many intersections in the ways of ongoing flux, places of steady but impermanent homeostasis.

These are called things.

> *Thing (Old English): an assembly, a gathering*
> *Thingan (Old English): to invite, to address*
> *Althing (Icelandic): the parliament*

An object is a thing that has been removed from its party line of rhizomes, hyphae, and roots, and treated to public scrutiny — framed, analyzed, experimented upon, known.

An object is a thing under surveillance.

Something is lost, some thing is lost, when a thing is made into an object.

We mourn the lost thing, even as we pursue the inescapable human work of objectification.

Homo faber tristis.

Man the creator — sad/foul smelling.
(as 2nd word of binomial name)

To Clasp

1.
Handhold-to-go, spare spine,
trail buddy, measure-minder,
prod: my palm, I trust,
will not forget you – aspen-soft
and slightly soapy, as though you'd paused,
musing, en route from wood to muscle
or vice versa. Nor will my arm and shoulder
lose the slight give you gave –
a shrug or nod –
as you took my sloughed-off weight.
Now retired, four-fifths fetishized,
you lean in my kitchen,
still wearing the duct tape I applied
that time I stepped back (eyes
loving only the bird in the binoculars)
and cracked you. Renewed apologies,
although you must admit
it did improve your flex,
and now you wear that silver wrap
as sash, not bandage.
                              Here's to us –
I raise my coffee cup –
here's to the brotherhood of sticks and bones.

2.
On a steep ascent
we made ourselves machinery,
plant and hoick, plant and hoick,
we hauled the species by its scruff,
by its gristle and thew,
up to the viewpoint.
Fording a creek you were the brace
that bore us, teetery,
over. Along a level trail
your swing-and-touch would
counterpoint the pace, now and then
pointing – a raised baton – toward some
rustle in the brush or an especially louche
lichen. Off duty, you'd lean on a trunk,
no doubt recalling an illustrious forebear –
the alpenstock, the crook,
the lever that could lift the world,
or the rod that smote the rock
to make the water flow –
while I regathered breath, reread the map,
and drank.

3.

How we met. 1986 or '87 it would be, and in that stretch of the
Pukaskwa Trail between Willow River and Oiseau Bay. What I
recall about that trip is the plainsong of warblers – yellow-rumped
ones *seedle seedling* and black-throated green ones *zoo zoo zee zoo
zeeing*, intercut, or pierced, by the sudden lyric reaches of white-
throated sparrows. That, and, of course, my knee going out, which
– as I remember it – translated that plainsong into little tone rows
of crankiness. I'd been limping along with a spruce pole, which was
rough and stiff and left black resin stains on my palm. Then the
path crossed a stream just below a beaver dam, and there you were,
ready to hand, trimmed and tidy, with your end chewed in the
beaver's classic wedge.

   In one version of the story I leave the beaver a token of my
appreciation, maybe a handful of trail mix or a pair of dirty socks
to plug the dam. But I just took you. It's not like there's a dearth
of aspen poplars or that beavers have gone off chewing them. And
it wasn't that I quit limping, more like the limp had someone it
could talk to, someone who'd receive the weight – that slight flex
– rather than just tolerating it like some stiff piece of spruce. By
the time we made it back to the car and trailhead, days later, you
had progressed from third to second person and we were like *that*,
closer than what's-his-name and Rin Tin Tin.

   Now fast-forward fifteen years or so, when I'm searching
for a lost logging locomotive (another story) in the bush up the
slope from the Strait of Juan de Fuca, and get lost myself. Not
on purpose, although you can imagine some sage or pseudo-sage
recommending behaving like a wolf to find a wolf, and getting lost
to find what's missing. I had paused to sit on a log and recover
my bearings when I realized I didn't know where the path was
any more than the alleged, probably mystical, logging locomotive.

I thrashed about some in the salmonberry and salal, and finally found a disused logging road, which in time took me back to the highway. It was only then that I realized that my stick – my trusty, second-personned, but interestingly still unnamed stick – wasn't with me. And do you think I could find my way back to that log? You don't get lost, the same pseudo-sage has probably said, lostness gets you. So that was that. The end.

Except it wasn't, as you have no doubt inferred from the fact that it's leaning against the wall in my kitchen. My friend Jane was in the habit of hiking up there, both for the exercise and to spy on Western Forest Products, who had flagged that patch for cutting. One day she was sitting on a log to rest, and, you guessed it, there, glinting like a jewel in the underbrush, was the duct tape on my stick. True story. And, as the narrator at the end of one of E. Nesbit's novels remarks, it's not his fault if it works out like Dickens, life just is like books sometimes. And I say, thank Raven for that.

4.

Back here amid the pots and pans
and precious bric-a-brac,
the Inuit soapstone loon,
the raw chunks of lava and peridotite,
and you, I think again.
How you must have grown,
one aspen in a clone of aspens,
a chorus of centuplets putting forth
your sticky buds and shedding spade-shaped leaves
in unison. Heaven,
some would say, a family tree
minus the fools, knaves, maiden aunts,
and history.
              From which we saved you –
first the beaver
with her riparian enhancement plans
then me with my bum knee.
And for these gifts of difference and distance,
and the *realpolitik* of use,
you may curse us or bless us or both.

Appropriate forms of address:

> *to objects: "We can do this the hard way, or we can do it the easy way..."*
>
> *to things: "I venture to enquire...."*

To Step

1.
Who will sustain these frail splayed
assemblages, with their knobs,
arches, tender soles,
their toes like droll noses
poking their little ways into the future?
Who will swaddle them against the cold,
brace them, gird them for the world of work,
and shield them from the errant ax?

                       Ah,

let there be boots.
Let them lurk in our sheds,
our vestibules, under our beds,
their mute tongues lolling,
their laces unstrung like Victorian corsets
wanting only to be worn.
May there be eros in our entries,
as the burrowing of moles more
snugly into earth.
And the lacing up:
let it be brisk, each cross
tugging the previous criss
taut. Then,
with our soles supported and our ankles hugged,
let them carry us – *andiamo!* –
out the door and up the ridge.

2.

After work we would sit around in the old farmhouse where we
lodged, drinking beer, playing cards, shooting the shit, smoking,
and dubbining our boots. We'd each bought a pair – Grebs or
Kingtreads – to mark this rite of passage into the working life and
out of the silly sneakers of youth. The dubbin restored grease to
the leather, making it more waterproof and suppler; it coaxed the
animal partly back to life. Surely concubines in harems were not
massaged more thoroughly, the toes, the insteps, the high uppers,
the secret, tucked-away tongues. Surely these pieces of hide were
no more cherished, or water repellent, when they'd been worn
by cows. Yes, the absence of girlfriends may have played a part in
the ritual, as our profane banter ("Looks like Danny's getting to
second base with his boots") did not fail to make explicit. But it
also involved the proud hands' homage to the humble feet, who
were proving to be far more sensitive, and important, than we'd
ever imagined back in the city.

Probably we were also trying to make our boots look more
worn than they really were, disguising their lack of nicks and
scratches – although these would accumulate soon enough. Each
time I pulled mine on (Grebs, light brown), I immediately wanted
to live up to them, the way an inexperienced rider wants to be
worthy of his horse. Their weight meant that each step was swung,
and the swing made momentum and the momentum returned the
foot to the ground, where it belonged, with some energy left over
for the next. They were like and unlike the hiking boots I've worn
in recent years, as a fiddle is like and unlike a violin.

In memory this occurs about three beats before the entry of
women and ambition as major themes. Manhood fully loaded but
aimless, innocent as a tornado or forest fire. When we walked up
the road to Tassé's for meals, our boots waited with the dogs on the

porch, a loose platoon, a pack, ready for work but equally open to suggestions. These generally meant pranks, which were elaborate and drastic, borrowing from the traditions of *commedia dell'arte* and vendetta, a daisy chain of linked reprisals featuring ambush, defenestration, and sudden buckets of water or paint. One found its dénouement in Emergency, followed by an epilogue delivered by the Director, the gist of which was the prank's exclusion, as a genre, of Mature Judgment, an element that could only enhance the quality and length of our as yet undistinguished existences. Words to that effect. He did not ask, as I do now, where we found the energy, after a day chopping and hauling brush, for spontaneous theatre. It was as though the very force that wore us out in work was winding up the mainspring of mischief, like the complementary spinning gyres in Yeats's cosmology.

While our boots waited outside, we'd have beans, boiled potatoes, sausages with maple syrup, tourtières on Sunday, Réjeanne bustling between the stove and the table, Julien presiding at its head as genially as he did on the job. After supper we'd spend long minutes sitting on the steps getting our boots back on, amicably arguing. Would we paddle up the creek to check on the beaver dam, or walk to the tavern in town? Each option plump with possibility, the birches reflected in the lake, the laces snubbed up tight, the Shadow just a shadow swelling under the trees.

Phenomenology is one name for the path back from the object to the thing, the counterbalance to objectification, or "progress." Poetry is another.

Rather than treading the one-way street of progress mythology, we may place ourselves on a ferry whose name alters each time it changes direction. On the outbound voyage it might be known as "Boldly Go" or "Cogito"; on the return "Mysterium" or "Francis Ponge" or "Nostos."

To Rock

1.
Rocks, you rock not. But when
you do, it's catastrophic.
Please don't. Be reliable St. Peter,
not the sudden shudderer,
not havocking spasmodic Loki
jerking in his chains.
Shake not, neither rattle,
nor roll your blunt tons downhill
on the village. Rather
let us dole you out in small
homeopathic doses fit to lull
our infants into sleep,
our old folk into memories:

> to and fro
> that wind not blow
> for now, the bough
> not break nor baby come to harm,
> that earth not quake,
> for now, for now,
> we rock our multi-purpose charm.

2.

And what about the to's and fro's
of this one, with its scarred arms,
backside-polished seat and sweater-snagging nails
forever poking up, its pronounced
slouch to the left, as though
each right angle wished it were obtuse?
Cocked back on its rockers,
it's an invitation that's a dare.
It says, not respite, not repose,
but *park your arse here, boy,*
I'm as rickety as you'll one day be,
hang on and hope. To rock here
sets that musical arthritis going –
insect chirps, the creak-work of a sailing ship,
the busy bush of ghosts.
Embraced by bricolage,
you ride that corpse-road, borne
in your coffin up the ridge
and over, hearing your pallbearers' groans
blend with your mother's as she
bore you in the opposite direction.

To rock here summons Angus
wielding his Tyrannosaurus chainsaw,
crooked knife, and plane, his profane
collection of knacks like near-accidents
whacked together. He is painting
the boreal bush over every part
except the seat – a river, with fisherman
and rapids, a porcine bear,

a moose, or mooselike antlered ungulate,
a forest fire, iconic Vs of geese.
And, tying them together, dotted daubs
and wavy lines like those, I've since read,
found in Neolithic caves.

All of this erased, in innocence,
by kind folk doing me, they thought,
a favour. Stripping furniture was all the rage
back then, to find the grain (ash,
in this case) and rescue pure form
from deplorable bad taste.
Let our rocking also summon
and forgive them, and myself,
for banishing it outdoors to the porch
where its blankness might grow bleaker in the weather.
Decades later, I came to relent,
and sanded off the funguslike accumulated scurf,
and wrote a rickety, heartfelt, verse-prose
gizmo with the rocking chair as muse.

So now to rock once more
calling forth, with our companionable creaks
whatever might be on our mind: another reprise
of the art of losing, I suspect,
how it's actually a bugger to pick up.
A god can't do it, brimful
of fullness as he fully is.
Now and then a poet's deft
recursive verse may coax
its absence into dance, its anguish

into recognition. But for daily use
a kitchen or a shed's the thing
with its native tools hanging on the walls,
a place where work meets art
for a palaver and a smoke, where Angus pauses,
paintbrush in the air,
deciding where to stick the moose.
Let's rock back there, and past it,
up the trail to the clearing
where he's pondering a large white ash,
the saw already growling in his grip,
and in his head – rendered transparent
by our trancelike to and fro – door frames,
paddles, firewood, and a fancy rocking chair.

V

Some day I will abandon them –
the old pine desk and comfortable sofa,
the broken walking stick and three-pairs-ago
superannuated boots, the leather lounger
like a catcher's mitt, the birch IKEA chair
that gives a little with your weight, as though
simply sitting were a softly lofted thought –
some day I'll leave this fine museum of effects
(*Shorter Oxford, OED*), and devote
what time is left to ferries, forth,
back, honouring the crossings, the betweens
I could not stand when I was someone going somewhere,
sort of, and forced them to conclude, or rather
come to rest, or rather
end. Now it's clear Achilles
isn't going to catch the tortoise,
though he'll leave a lot of items disassembled
in his wake. Things come apart
so easily, and like the sign says,
you break it, it's yours.
You take it home, maimed, wonky,
missing a knob or leg, to convalesce
for the duration on a shelf. Now it's
so long precious *choses*, I'm off
to Bell Island, Battle Harbour, Harris,
Heimay. That's me,
leaning on the rail, searching with binoculars –
if I've forgotten not to bring them –

for dolphins, gannets, or the chalk-white cliffs.
There I am – the darling of Ephemeros,
my knapsack stuffed with ticket stubs
and trail bar wrappers, schedules for ferries
in the Baltic, the Aegean, and the Inside
Passage. Between one and the next
I'll go on foot, no, donkey, no, I'll hitch rides
with undertakers, cemetery to cemetery, my ear open
to his argot of real estate, The Heart Fund,
and the benefits of planning for that Sad
Inevitable Day. That's me, feasting on cliché,
cultivating ennui and a thirst so fine
I make a beeline for the next boat's lounge
and drink my way to Ilfracombe and back
with Dylan Thomas, to and fro to Staten Island
drink for drink with Lowell on a bender – or,
better – head for Port-aux-Basques or Blanc-Sablon
with manic homebound Newfoundland-and-Labradorians,
jigs and reels unscrolling like a casually
opened vein.
           And that's me, later,
lurching the deck, radar-gazing the waves
that blitz us out of darkness, shock troops
for the infinite. And will I know it
when I board the last one?
Will it wear its beauty cleanly
as a bluenose or a shark, remorseless music
slicing the tickle or the gulf? Or will it
slouch its rusted ancient people-smuggling hull
up to the pier, still reeking of accumulated pain?
I imagine one of B.C. Ferries' floating wedding cakes

refit to match Miss Havisham's, or the *Titanic*
with its band still playing and its rhetoric
reversed. Maybe I will know it by the sad
unburied throng that's waiting at the terminal,
maundering the boardwalk, snoozing in cars,
re-browsing postcards, key chains, stuffed puffins,
chocolate moose turds, patrolling the lined-up idling
rhinestoned eighteen-wheelers, the Windstar
with its indefatigably yapping poodle, the flock
of lounging Harley-Davidsons like decadent
black sheep, all of us picking up one minute,
putting it down, picking up the next
in serial et cetera.
                    One thing's for sure:
when its skipper finally
steps out on the bridge, he or she steps
straight from déjà vu. So it was you,
all along, we'll each exclaim, whoozit, buddy,
the one I never recognized but somehow knew,
that patched grey cloak, that slept-in suit,
that face at once a road map and a lava flow,
I should have known, we groan,
as each, laboriously,
climbs aboard.

DESCENT

In the end
he leaves the difficult lyre
behind and clambers down, handhold
by outcrop by ledge,
shedding talent, fame
fading like a tan. Angel,
artist. His head
humbled by its skull.
Apprentice. Among such
gravities to find himself again
ungainly. Thrawn. The country-and-
western singer whose sad similes
come home to roost. Like doves.
Like crows. Like
chickens. His theme park.
His menagerie. Once his song
made rocks move and the gods
relent.
Such was the boast.
Now the rocks
rub raw the bone. Gravel,
scree. Who will name
the dark's own instrument? Riprap,
slag. Music
tearing itself apart.

NOTES

Page

1   "As If": Pouch Cove, Newfoundland.

8   Forlorn! the very word is like a bell
        To toll me back from thee to my sole self!
            – John Keats, "Ode to a Nightingale"

11   Mount Work: Victoria, B.C.

17   "On the Barrens": Southeast Avalon Peninsula,
        Newfoundland.

        harrier: a.k.a. marsh hawk.

        goowiddy: a.k.a. sheep laurel, a.k.a. *Kalmia angustifolia*.

19   "Alias Rabbit, Alias Snowshoe Hare": Northeast Avalon
        Peninsula, Newfoundland.

21   "Porch": Glengarry County, Ontario.

23   "Sleeping with the River": Campbell River, B.C.

24   tolt: a prominent rounded hill.

        volcaniclastic: cf. "Tuff," page 44.

erratic: a rock carried by a glacier and left in a new location, where it often contrasts with the surrounding rock formations.

CFA: literally "come from away"; allochthonous.

27   imperial canoe trips: Duncan Campbell Scott, one of the Confederation Poets and an agent for the Department of Indian Affairs, made several treaty-making canoe trips in Northern Ontario bribing Ojibwa and Cree people to concede their land. See Stan Dragland, *Floating Voice* (Toronto: House of Anansi Press, 1994).

Norval Morrisseau: Ojibwa artist and shaman.

29   "Apparition": Southeast Avalon Peninsula, Newfoundland.

31   *Sleeping Places, Newfoundland 1982*: an artwork by Marlene Creates comprised of twenty-five black-and-white photographs of ground she slept on around the island of Newfoundland.

35   Epigraph from Robert Hass, "State of the Planet," in *Time and Materials* (New York: Ecco Press, 2007).

36   schiller: the visual effect produced, as in Labradorite, when light is reflected inside the rock before being reflected back out.

The Land God Gave to Cain: Labrador, as described by Jacques Cartier.

38   Mistaken Point: site of rare Ediacaran fossils on the Avalon Peninsula of Newfoundland. These fossils are evidence of the oldest known animals, or proto-animals, on Earth. Discoveries at Mistaken Point, Ediacara in Australia, and Arkangel in Russia have instigated the establishment of a new geologic period called the Ediacaran, preceding the Cambrian.

Anthropocene: proposed designation for the current epoch.

39   *Paradoxides*: This genus of trilobite serves as an index fossil both temporally and spatially. It identifies a formation as Mid-Cambrian, since it existed during that relatively brief period, 520 million years ago. Spatially, the presence of a *Paradoxides* fossil like the one we found that day identifies landmasses that were formerly part of a micro-continent called Avalonia. During much of the Paleozoic era, Avalonia existed as a separate island in the middle of the Iapetus Ocean (the Atlantic's predecessor), and so developed species unique to itself, rather like the species that are unique to Australia today. Remnants of Avalonia, as established by *Paradoxides* fossils and other evidence in the rock sequences, include all of the Avalon Peninsula, and parts of Wales, Ireland, New Brunswick, and Massachusetts.

Cephalon, thorax, and *pygidium*: the head, body, and tail of a trilobite.

41   *Thorax*: quotations, in italic, are drawn from the *Oxford English Dictionary*; Richard Fortey's *Trilobite* (New

York: Vintage, 2001); Søren Kierkegaard's *Practice in Christianity*, translated by H.V. Hong and Edna Hong (Princeton, N.J.: Princeton University Press, 1991); Christopher Dewdney's "Grid Erectile," in *Predators of the Adoration* (Toronto: McClelland & Stewart, 1983); and Meng Hao-jan's "Listening to Cheng Yin Play His Ch'in," translated by David Hinton, in *The Mountain Poems of Meng Hao-jan* (Brooklyn, N.Y.: Archipelago Books, 2004).

42   Allochthon and autochthon: originating elsewhere and originating in the place currently found, respectively. Cf. CFA, above.

44   "Tuff": Portugal Cove, Newfoundland.

Tuff is rock formed from compressed volcanic ash and other debris from eruptions.

46   Snowball Earth: This hypothesis, which has gained increasing credence among geologists, postulates that Earth was entirely (or mostly, depending on the theorist) covered in ice for 100 million years in the late Proterozoic Era. The evidence includes the discovery of formations dating from 750 to 600 million years ago that show the traces of strong glaciation combined with origins at or near the equator.

One problem posed by the Snowball Earth hypothesis was the issue of Earth's return to seasonal cycles, once winter had become absolute. This is addressed in the last stanza of section I on pages 46–47.

ultramafic: mafic rocks are igneous rocks that are high

in magnesium and iron, like basalt. Ultramafic rocks are especially so, having their origins in the mantle of the planet. Peridotite, such as that found in the Tablelands in Gros Morne National Park, is an example of a rare appearance of ultramafic rocks on the surface.

albedo: the reflection of the sun's rays back into space by ice fields and glaciers, as opposed to their absorption by oceans and rocks.

48   "Rock Flour": Kluane National Park, Yukon.

katabatic wind: wind descending from a glacier.

Beringia: name given to the area around the current Bering Sea, which was ice-free during the last ice age. It included what is now the bottom of the Bering Strait, which afforded a land bridge between Asia and North America.

49   Crinoid: an echinoderm of the class Crinodea, a.k.a. sea lilies, dating from the Ordovician to the present. Their segmented stalks resemble, but are unrelated to, the vertebrae of chordates such as ourselves.

50   "Gjall": Snæfellsnes Peninsula, Iceland.

Gjall is a very light rock formed when lava solidifies while flying through the air during an eruption.

51   Wopmay Orogen: An orogen is a mountain-building episode in Earth's history. The remains of the Wopmay

Orogen, which occurred about two billion years ago, lie in the tundra of the Northwest Territories between Great Bear Lake and Coronation Gulf on the Arctic Ocean. The sequence of rock formations in the Wopmay Orogen is the same as those shown in modern orogenies such as the Rockies, the Andes, and the Himalayas.

molasse: a rock formation composed of sediments eroded from mountains following an orogeny.

56   *homo faber tristis*: man the sad maker.

61   clone: a group of organisms, such as a grove of aspen poplars, deriving from a single individual by asexual means. Aspen clones are among the oldest, as well as the largest, organisms in the world. See John Laird Farrar, *Trees in Canada* (Markham, Ont.: Fitzhenry & Whiteside and Canadian Forest Service, 1995).

69   gizmo: "Sanding Down This Rocking Chair on a Windy Night" in the book by the same title (Toronto: McClelland & Stewart, 1987).

74   Ephemeros: god of trivia, the unregarded, and mayflies.

ACKNOWLEDGEMENTS

Some of these poems have appeared in the following periodicals and anthologies: *Riddle Fence, The Fiddlehead, The Review, The Malahat Review, Pith and Wry,* and *The Best Canadian Poetry* for 2008 and 2009.

"Thingamajig" is a version of a piece commissioned by David Maggs as part of his project "The Implicated Subject" – a contribution to Vancouver's "Greenest City Conversation."

Thanks to all those who lent an ear: Mark Abley, Marlene Creates, Mary Dalton, Stan Dragland, Tim Lilburn, Sally McKay, and Jan Zwicky; and to those who lent valuable geological advice and assistance: Doug Boyce, Julie Cappleman, Paul Dean, Liam Herringshaw, and Richard Thomas.

My gratitude to Rob Vanderheyden for the excellent photograph of the *Paradoxides* fossil, and Anita Chong at McClelland & Stewart for her care and patience in guiding its namesake through to press.

Most especially I want to acknowledge the editorial acumen of my owl-eared editor, Barry Dempster.